BISCOTTI

BISCOTTI

Lou Seibert Pappas

Illustrations by Piet Halberstadt

CHRONICLE BOOKS

SAN FRANCISCO

Library of Congress Cataloging-in-Publication Data:

Pappas, Lou Seibert.
    Biscotti / by Lou Seibert Pappas : illustrated by Piet Halberstadt.
        p. cm.
    ISBN 0-8118-0095-4
    1. Cookies. 2. Cookery, Italian. I. Title.
TX772.P26 1992   91-33884
841.8'654—dc20   CIP

Printed in Hong Kong

ISBN 0-8118-0095-4

Distributed in Canada by Raincoast Books
8680 Cambie Street, Vancouver, B.C. V6P 6M9

20 19 18 17 16 15 14 13

Chronicle Books
85 Second Street
San Francisco, CA 94105

www.chroniclebooks.com

Contents

Introduction

Bravo biscotti! These tantalizing twice-baked Italian cookies are the new darling of confections. Their stellar rise to fame comes naturally. With each bite they shatter into teasing goodness, prompting another morsel.

Subtly sweet and ultra-crispy, they make a seductive snack at any time of day. Traditionally in Tuscany, Italians favor them as dipping cookies, to dunk in wine, but their savoring possibilities are limitless from dawn to dusk. With their myriad flavor combinations, they are a delight at any hour and slip into all occasions: the breakfast routine, a lunchtime sweet, a cappuccino accompaniment, a gelato partner, and a late-night snack with hot chocolate or port.

The word *biscotti* actually has a double meaning. The root name stems from *bis* and *cotto*. *Bis* translates to "more than one" and *cotto* means "cooking" in Italian. This is achieved by forming the dough into logs and baking once; then the baked strips are sliced diagonally and returned to the oven for a second baking.

The name *biscotti* is also a generic term denoting various types of Italian cookies. Italian pasticcerie, or pastry shops, flaunt biscotti like a banner across the exterior of their shops, alerting customers to cookies in all styles. Many are big and chunky, loaded with whole nuts or sugar crystals, with an earthy home-made look. Cylindrical glass jars often hold the nut-studded oblong wafers that we know as biscotti in the States. Chock-full of almonds, hazelnuts, pine nuts, citron or raisins, these cookies also come in many flavor variations in Italy, traditionally cut short and stubby, about 3 to 4 inches long.

The quintessential biscotti are said to be the Biscotti di Prato. In Tuscany two decades ago, they were a Florentine discovery for me, along with the exquisite gelati and semi-freddi from the gelateria Perche No, where zabaione, spumone, pistachio nut, gianduia and rum praline were among the tiny scoops mounded high in a paper cup. And from a nearby pasticceria a bagful of the ultra-crisp, not-too-sweet Biscotti di Prato made an irresistible mate with the frosty lickings.

Much later I learned that Biscotti di Prato are crisp, dry almond biscuits named for the city of Prato, located about 15 kilometers from Florence. Twice-baked and almond-strewn, they were a 14th-century creation of Datini, a gourmet of the era. They were served then as now with a glass of Vin Santo, meaning holy wine, for dunking. A dry to sweet Tuscan wine with a golden-brown hue, it is not fortified with extra alcohol, yet reminiscent of sherry and port in depth of flavor and sweetness. Dipping a cookie in a glass makes a synergistic pairing, a mouth-filling taste far greater than either one alone, claim aficionados.

Elsewhere in Italy, particularly Sicily, anise-flavored biscuits mate with *caffelatte* (coffee with hot milk) as an everyday breakfast food, replacing bread. Traditionally an Italian classic, biscotti have been baked for centuries. According to some historians, Venetian pani biscotti were a perfect provision for sailors and even businessmen who went to sea for months at a time. The biscuits were thoroughly baked to draw off almost all their moisture and produced a light cracker-like ration that couldn't possibly mold. Christopher Columbus relied on biscotti on long sea voyages, and

English sailors had hardtack in their diet in the days when Britannia's sailing ships ruled the waves.

Other nationalities have created cousins to this cookie. Jewish mandelbrot, Dutch rusk, German zwieback, Greek paxemadia, and even British hardtack, are related, with their double baking criteria that makes them crisp and long-lasting. However, today's versions are far more sophisticated than the ancient ones.

American purveyors have revived this beloved cookie, and now dozens of firms are baking and shipping artistically designed bagfuls nationwide along with marketing imported biscotti. With spiraling competition, new flavors have been introduced. Taking liberties with the biscotti formula is a winning opportunity. All sorts of nuts, fruits, extracts and liqueurs can enhance them. Instead of producing the original stubby cookies, they can be sliced diagonally into 6-inch-long stylish oblongs. The possibilities are unlimited.

This collection expands on the biscotti philosophy with 26 delectable flavors. Cioccolato, Nocciole, Pignoli and Gianduia are superb plain. Others are frosted with a chocolate veneer. A passion for ginger prompts a triple dose; an addiction for praline spurs a candy-like biscuit; a search for the healthful creates a granola style.

Today Americans are embracing this Italian dessert with a soaring passion. There's a style for every palate. Low in fat and sugar and, in most versions, calories as well, biscotti are being pegged as the cookie of the 90's and challenging chocolate chip cookies in popularity.

Biscotti Baking Tips

Baking biscotti at home is quick and easy. Equipment is minimal. A bowl and a spoon, or a mixer, and a baking sheet are the only essentials. It takes just 15 minutes to mix up the dough and shape logs and another brief span of time for cutting them diagonally at a 45-degree angle for the second baking to dry them further. A brimming tinful that keeps for weeks (if hidden from the passionate) is the delectable result.

Hints for Success
Measure ingredients accurately.

Lightly salted butter was used in testing these recipes, but you may substitute unsalted butter. A high-quality firm margarine may also be used although it will not give the same flavor as butter.

Mix just until the dough clings together; do not overwork it.

Shape dough into logs with clean, lightly floured hands. If hands become sticky with dough, clean them and re-flour. The dough will be sticky.

For easy removal and cleanup, the baking sheet may be lined with parchment, but it is not essential.

A serrated knife works well for slicing.

Chocolate is listed by weight. For a dry measure equivalent, 3 ounces chopped chocolate equals ½ cup, or 4 ounces chopped chocolate equals

²/₃ cup. Chocolate melts at 98.6 degrees, so heat over simmering, not boiling water. Avoid steam as moisture causes chocolate to seize or cling together.

Watch the baking of biscotti carefully. Check cookies for signs of doneness prior to the suggested baking time as every oven bakes differently.

Let baked logs cool a few minutes before slicing diagonally on a cutting board with firm, decisive strokes, to prevent crumbling.

Return sliced cookies to the oven lying cut-side down if a crispy surface is desired or standing upright for simply drying the cookie, especially if it contains chocolate or dried fruit.

Let the cookies cool completely on the pan or a rack before storing in a tightly closed container. Let chocolate-frosted biscotti stand at room temperature to firm up. Refrigerating them causes the chocolate to turn grayish white in color.

If cookies are overly dry, place them in a paper bag and let them sit at room temperature to age for a few days so they may absorb a little moisture from the air and soften.

Cookies keep well stored in a tin at room temperature for a few weeks.

Cookies can be tightly wrapped in freezer paper and a plastic bag and frozen, but should be eaten within a month as flavor diminishes.

Cookies may be reheated in a 300 degree oven for 10 to 15 minutes to freshen the flavor.

Serving Ideas with Biscotti

Crumbled cookies, especially the drier, ultra-crisp styles, such as Biscotti di Prato or Biscotti al Cioccolato, are excellent sprinkled over ice cream or frozen yogurt. Try them on such flavors as vanilla bean, Kona coffee, chocolate or toasted almond. If desired, drizzle a spoonful of liqueur such as Amaretto, Frangelico, Grand Marnier or cognac on top.

To make a quick crust for an ice cream pie, scatter crushed Granola Biscotti over a pie pan, press in coffee ice cream, and serve with warm fudge sauce.

Pour champagne or sparkling wine over a fresh fruit goblet of straw-berries, sliced peaches or nectarines as a sumptuous mate to Biscotti alle Mandorle or Almond Crunch Biscotti.

Wholesome cookies, such as Fruited Nut Biscotti, Granola Biscotti, and Pistachio and Golden Raisin Biscotti, are apropos for breakfast.

Biscotti make charming personal gifts for friends or neighbors. Package them in a plastic bag and tie with a ribbon or give in a decorative tin container.

Offer an assortment of biscotti for a buffet party, including a variety of types: classic Italian, chocolate, fruited and spicy.

TRADITIONAL

Biscotti Toscani

With a delicate flavor, these are an all-around cookie—ideal for savoring plain or with ice cream, frozen yogurt or cappuccino.

Place nuts in a shallow pan and bake in a preheated 325 degree oven until golden brown, about 8 to 10 minutes. Let cool. In a mixing bowl cream butter and sugar until light and fluffy. Beat in eggs, vanilla, almond extract and orange zest. In a bowl combine the flour, baking powder, nutmeg and salt. Add to the creamed mixture, mixing until blended. Cut almonds into halves or thirds and fold in. Divide dough in half. Place on a greased and floured baking sheet and form into two logs about 1/2 inch thick, 1 1/2 inches wide and 12 inches long, spacing them at least 2 inches apart. Bake in the middle of a preheated 325 degree oven for 25 minutes or until a light golden brown. Transfer from the baking sheet to a rack. Let cool 5 minutes. Place on a cutting board. With a serrated knife slice diagonally at a 45 degree angle about 1/2 inch thick. Lay the slices flat on the baking sheet and return to the oven for 10 minutes, turning them over once, to dry slightly. Let cool on a rack. Store in a tightly covered container.

Makes 3 1/2 dozen biscotti.

1/2 cup whole almonds

1/3 cup butter

3/4 cup sugar

2 eggs

1 teaspoon vanilla extract

1/4 teaspoon almond extract

2 teaspoons grated orange zest

2 1/4 cups all-purpose flour

1 1/2 teaspoons baking powder

1/8 teaspoon nutmeg

1/4 teaspoon salt

Biscotti di Prato

¾ *cup whole almonds*

3 eggs

1 teaspoon vanilla

¼ teaspoon almond extract

2 cups unbleached or all-purpose flour

⅞ *cup sugar*

1 teaspoon baking soda

Dash of salt

A perfect accompaniment to espresso or cappuccino, this classical Italian dunking cookie is traditional to the Tuscany region, where it is usually served with a glass of Vin Santo.

Place nuts in a shallow pan and bake in a preheated 350 degree oven for 8 to 10 minutes, or until golden brown. Let cool. In a small bowl beat eggs, vanilla and almond extract with a wire whisk. In a mixing bowl combine flour, sugar, baking soda and salt. Add egg mixture and mix until blended, about 1 minute. Cut nuts into halves or thirds and mix in. Divide dough in half. On a greased and floured baking sheet, pat out dough into two logs about ½ inch thick, 1½ inches wide and 12 inches long, spacing them at least 2 inches apart. Bake in the middle of a preheated 300 degree oven for 50 minutes or until golden brown. Transfer from the baking sheet to a rack. Let cool 5 minutes. Place on a cutting board. With a serrated knife slice diagonally at a 45 degree angle about ½ inch thick. Lay the slices flat on the baking sheet and return to a 275 degree oven for 20 to 25 minutes or until toasted, turning them over once to dry the other side. Store in a tightly covered container.

Chocolate Glaze variation. Coarsely chop 3 ounces semisweet chocolate and place in a small pan that fits snugly over a saucepan of barely simmering water. Heat until chocolate melts. Stir to blend. Or place chocolate in a microwave-safe bowl and microwave on medium for 2 minutes or until chocolate melts. Stir to blend. With a spatula spread over entire top surface of cookies. Let cool at room temperature until set.

Makes about 3 1/2 dozen.

Biscotti alle Mandorle

¾ cup whole almonds

½ cup almond paste

3 eggs

¾ cup sugar

2 teaspoons grated lemon zest

½ teaspoon almond extract

1⅔ cups unbleached or all-purpose flour

⅓ cup cornstarch

½ teaspoon baking powder

¼ teaspoon salt

Almond paste lends its nutty sweetness to these sponge cake–like biscotti fingers.

Place nuts in a shallow pan and bake in a preheated 350 degree oven for 8 to 10 minutes, or until golden brown. Let cool. In a mixing bowl beat almond paste with a wire whisk until creamy. Beat in eggs. Gradually add sugar and beat until light and fluffy. Add lemon zest and almond extract. In a bowl combine the flour, cornstarch, baking powder and salt. Add to the egg mixture, mixing until blended. Cut nuts into halves or thirds and fold in. With a spatula spread the soft dough on a greased, floured baking sheet, forming two strips about 14 inches long and 2½ inches wide, spacing them at least 2 inches apart. Bake in the middle of a preheated 350 degree oven for 18 to 20 minutes or until golden brown. Transfer from the baking sheet to a rack. Let cool 5 minutes. Place on a cutting board. With a serrated knife slice diagonally at a 45 degree angle about ½ inch thick. Lay the slices flat on the baking sheet and return to a 325 degree oven for 10 minutes, turning them over once, to dry slightly.

Makes about 4 dozen.

Biscotti all' Anice

Imbued with a hint of anise, these cookies have a fine, almost silken texture. They are superb at any time of day.

Place nuts in a shallow pan and bake in a preheated 350 degree oven for 8 to 10 minutes, or until golden brown. Let cool. Place anise seeds in a small bowl. Add 1 tablespoon liqueur and heat in a 350 degree oven for 5 minutes to infuse. Or place anise seeds in a small microwave-safe bowl. Add 1 tablespoon liqueur and microwave on high for 10 to 15 seconds, or until steaming. Set aside. In a mixing bowl cream butter and sugar until light and fluffy. Beat in eggs. Add anise seed mixed with liqueur and the remaining 1 tablespoon liqueur. In a bowl combine the flour, baking powder and salt. Add to the creamed mixture, mixing just until blended. Cut nuts in halves or thirds and fold in. Divide dough in half. On a greased and floured baking sheet pat out into two logs about 1/2 inch high, 1 1/2 inches wide and 14 inches long, spacing at least 2 inches apart. Bake in the middle of a preheated 325 degree oven for 25 minutes or until lightly browned. Transfer from the baking sheet to a rack. Let cool for 5 minutes. Place on a cutting board. With a serrated knife slice at a 45 degree angle about 1/2 inch thick. Place the slices upright 1/2 inch apart on the baking sheet and return to the oven for 10 minutes longer to dry slightly. Let cool on a rack. Store in a tightly covered container.

Makes about 3 1/2 to 4 dozen.

2/3 cup whole almonds

1 tablespoon anise seeds

2 tablespoons Sambucca liqueur or Pernod

1/2 cup butter

3/4 cup sugar

2 eggs

2 cups plus 2 tablespoons unbleached or all-purpose flour

1 1/2 teaspoons baking powder

1/4 teaspoon salt

Pignoli Biscotti

2/3 cup pine nuts

1/2 cup butter

3/4 cup sugar

2 eggs

2 tablespoons lemon juice

2 tablespoons lemon zest

2 cups plus 2 tablespoons
unbleached or all-purpose
flour

1 1/2 teaspoons baking
powder

1/4 teaspoon salt

*With a nutty sweetness of pine nuts and fresh tang of lemon zest,
these are delightful all-around biscotti for snacking.*

Place nuts in a shallow pan and bake in a 350 degree oven for
6 to 8 minutes, or until golden brown. Let cool. In a mixing bowl
cream butter and sugar until light and fluffy. Beat in eggs, lemon
juice and zest. In a bowl combine the flour, baking powder and
salt. Add to the creamed mixture, mixing until blended. Fold in
nuts. Divide dough in half. On a greased and floured baking sheet
pat out into two logs about 1/2 inch high, 1 1/2 inches wide and
14 inches long, spacing them at least 2 inches apart. Bake in the
middle of a preheated 325 degree oven for 25 minutes or until
lightly browned. Transfer from the baking sheet to a rack. Let
cool for 5 minutes. Place on a cutting board. With a serrated
knife slice diagonally at a 45 degree angle about 1/2 inch thick.
Lay the slices flat on the baking sheet and return to the oven for
10 minutes longer, turning them over once, to dry slightly. Let
cool on a rack. Store in a tightly covered container.

Makes about 3 1/2 to 4 dozen.

CHOCOLATE

Double Chocolate Decadence
23

Biscotti Nocciole-Cioccolato
24

Chocolate Ribboned Biscotti
25

Biscotti al Cioccolato
26

Cioccolato Paradiso
28

Biscotti Gianduia
30

White Chocolate Macadamia Biscotti
32

& NUTS

Double Chocolate Decadence

Flecked with milk chocolate and almonds, these crispy biscotti have a rich chocolate flavor.

Place nuts in a shallow pan and bake in a preheated 350 degree oven for 8 to 10 minutes, or until golden brown. Let cool. In a mixing bowl cream butter and sugar until light and fluffy. Beat in eggs and liqueur or coffee. In a bowl combine the flour, cocoa, baking powder and salt. Add to the creamed mixture, mixing until blended. Cut nuts into halves or thirds. Fold in nuts and milk chocolate. Divide dough in half. On a greased and floured baking sheet pat out into two logs about $1/2$ inch high, $1 1/2$ inches wide and 14 inches long, spacing them at least 2 inches apart. Bake in the middle of a preheated 325 degree oven for 25 minutes or until lightly browned. Transfer from the baking sheet to a rack. Let cool for 5 minutes. Place on a cutting board. With a serrated knife slice diagonally on a 45 degree angle about $1/2$ inch thick. Place the slices upright on the baking sheet $1/2$ inch apart and return to the oven for about 8 to 10 minutes longer to dry slightly. Let cool on a rack. Store in a tightly covered container.

Makes about $3 1/2$ to 4 dozen.

$2/3$ cup whole almonds

$1/2$ cup butter

$3/4$ cup sugar

2 eggs

2 tablespoons Amaretto or Kahlua or double-strength coffee

2 cups plus 2 tablespoons unbleached or all-purpose flour

$1/3$ cup unsweetened cocoa

$1 1/2$ teaspoons baking powder

$1/4$ teaspoon salt

$2/3$ cup chopped milk chocolate

Biscotti Nocciole-Cioccolato

¾ cup hazelnuts

4 ounces bittersweet
chocolate

½ cup butter

¾ cup sugar

2 eggs

2 tablespoons Frangelico
or Amaretto

2 cups unbleached or all-
purpose flour

1½ teaspoons baking
powder

¼ teaspoon salt

*Chocolate shavings and hazelnuts contribute a double flavor impact
in this seductive variation.*

Place nuts in a shallow pan and bake in a preheated 350 degree
oven for 8 to 10 minutes, or until golden brown. Let cool. With
paper towels, rub nuts while warm to remove papery skins. Let
cool. In a food processor fitted with a steel blade, grind nuts
finely. Remove and set aside. Add the chocolate to the food
processor and process until coarsely ground. In a mixing bowl
cream butter and sugar until light and fluffy. Beat in eggs and
liqueur. In a bowl combine the flour, baking powder and salt .
Add to the creamed mixture, mixing until blended. Fold in nuts
and chocolate. Divide dough in half. On a greased and floured
baking sheet pat out into two logs about ½ inch high, 1½ inches
wide and 14 inches long, spacing them at least 2 inches apart. Bake
in the middle of a preheated 325 degree oven for 25 minutes or
until lightly browned. Transfer from the baking sheet to a rack.
Let cool for 5 minutes. Place on a cutting board. With a serrated
knife slice diagonally on a 45 degree angle about ½ inch thick.
Place the slices upright ½ inch apart on the baking sheet and
return to the oven for 10 minutes longer to dry slightly. Let cool
on a rack. Store in a tightly covered container.

Makes about 3½ to 4 dozen.

Chocolate Ribboned Biscotti

Use a top quality imported or domestic chocolate for these captivating biscotti.

Place nuts in a shallow pan and bake in a preheated 350 degree oven for 8 to 10 minutes, or until golden brown. Let cool. In a mixing bowl cream butter and sugar until light and fluffy. Beat in eggs, vanilla and almond extract. In a bowl combine the flour, baking powder and salt. Add to the creamed mixture, mixing until blended. Cut nuts into halves or thirds and fold in. Divide dough in half. On a greased and floured baking sheet pat out into two logs about 1/2 inch high, 1 1/2 inches wide and 14 inches long, spacing them at least 2 inches apart. Bake in the middle of a pre-heated 325 degree oven for 25 minutes or until lightly browned. Remove from baking sheet to a rack. Let cool for 5 minutes. Place on a cutting board. With a serrated knife slice diagonally at a 45 degree angle about 1/2 inch thick. Place the slices upright 1/2 inch apart on the baking sheet and return to the oven for 10 minutes longer to dry slightly. Let cool on a rack. Coarsely chop chocolate and place in a small bowl that fits tightly over a pan of barely simmering water. Heat until melted. Stir to blend. Or place chocolate in a microwave-safe bowl and microwave on medium for 2 minutes, or until melted. Stir to blend. With a spatula spread chocolate over entire top surface of cookies. Let cool at room temperature until set. Store in a tightly covered container.

Makes about 3 1/2 to 4 dozen.

2/3 cup whole almonds

1/2 cup butter

3/4 cup sugar

2 eggs

1 teaspoon vanilla

1/2 teaspoon almond extract

2 cups plus 2 tablespoons unbleached or all-purpose flour

1 teaspoon baking powder

1/4 teaspoon baking soda

1/4 teaspoon salt

3 ounces bittersweet chocolate

Biscotti al Cioccolato

¾ cup hazelnuts

3 eggs

1 teaspoon vanilla extract

¼ teaspoon almond extract

1 ¾ cups unbleached or all-purpose flour

¾ cup sugar

⅓ cup unsweetened cocoa

1 tablespoon powdered coffee

1 teaspoon baking soda

Dash of salt

These ultra-crisp chocolate cookies are akin to the Tuscan version called Biscotti di Prato. They are great dunkers and are wonderful with a goblet of vanilla bean or coffee ice cream. At Florian, one of the most popular and oldest Venetian cafes, biscotti flavored with chocolate, raisins or glacéed fruit are dipped in a glass of grappa liqueur.

Place nuts in a shallow pan and bake in a preheated 350 degree oven for 8 to 10 minutes, or until golden brown. While still warm, rub nuts between a double layer of paper towels to remove the

papery skins. Let cool. In a small bowl beat eggs, vanilla and almond extract with a wire whisk. In a mixing bowl combine flour, sugar, cocoa, coffee powder, baking soda and salt. Add egg mixture and mix until blended, about 1 minute. Fold in the nuts. Divide dough in half. On a greased and floured baking sheet, pat

out dough into two logs about ¹/₂ inch thick, 1 ¹/₂ inches wide and 12 inches long, spacing them at least 2 inches apart. Bake in the middle of a preheated 300 degree oven for 50 minutes or until set and baked through. Transfer from the baking sheet to a rack. Let cool 5 minutes. Place on a cutting board. With a serrated knife slice diagonally at a 45 degree angle about ¹/₂ inch thick. Lay the slices flat on the baking sheet and return to a 275 degree oven for 20 to 25 minutes, turning them over once, to dry slightly. Let cool on a rack. Store in a tightly covered container.

Chocolate Glaze variation. Coarsely chop 3 ounces of bittersweet chocolate and place in a small bowl that fits snugly over a saucepan of barely simmering water. Heat until melted. Stir to blend. Or place chocolate in a small microwave-safe bowl and microwave on medium for 2 minutes or until chocolate melts. Stir to blend. With a spatula spread chocolate over entire top surface of cookies. Let cool at room temperature until set.

Makes about 3 ¹/₂ dozen.

Cioccolato Paradiso

1 1/2 cups almonds

1/2 cup butter

1 cup plus 2 tablespoons sugar

3 eggs, separated

1 1/2 teaspoons vanilla extract

Zest of 1 orange, finely chopped

3 cups all-purpose or unbleached flour

2 teaspoons baking powder

1/4 teaspoon salt

1 1/4 cups coarsely chopped milk chocolate

Milk chocolate chunks and toasty almonds stud these orange-scented biscotti for a delectable flavor harmony.

Place nuts in a shallow pan and bake in a preheated 350 degree oven for 8 to 10 minutes, or until golden brown. Let cool. In a mixing bowl cream butter and 1/2 cup sugar until light and fluffy. Beat in egg yolks, vanilla and orange zest. In a bowl combine the flour, baking powder and salt. Add to the creamed mixture, mixing just until crumbly. In a separate bowl beat egg whites until soft peaks form and beat in remaining sugar, beating until stiff but not dry. Fold meringue into the crumbly dough, mixing until it clings together. Cut nuts into halves or thirds and fold in along with chocolate. Divide dough in half. Form into two logs on a greased and floured baking sheet making them about 1/2 inch thick, 1 1/2 inches wide and 16 inches long, spacing them at least 2 inches apart. Bake in the middle of a preheated 325 degree oven for 25 minutes or until set and golden brown. Transfer from the baking sheet to a rack. Let cool 5 minutes. Place on a cutting board. With a serrated knife slice diagonally at a 45 degree angle about 1/2 inch thick. Place the slices upright on a baking sheet and return to the oven at 300 degrees for 10 to 15 minutes to dry slightly. Let cool on a rack. Store in a tightly covered container.

Makes about 4 dozen.

Biscotti Gianduia

½ cup each hazelnuts and almonds

5 ounces unsweetened chocolate

½ cup butter

1 cup sugar

3 eggs

½ teaspoon vanilla extract

2 tablespoons Frangelico liqueur or double-strength coffee

3 cups plus 2 tablespoons unbleached or all-purpose flour

1½ teaspoons baking powder

¼ teaspoon salt

On an early trip to Italy, sampling gelato became a rapturous daily escapade. One of the most seductive flavors is gianduia, with its mingling of chocolate, hazelnuts and almonds. Here it inspires this flavor combination.

Place hazelnuts and almonds in separate shallow pans and bake in a preheated 350 degree oven for 8 to 10 minutes, or until golden brown. While still warm, rub hazelnuts between a double layer of paper towels to remove the papery skins. Let cool. Coarsely chop chocolate and place in a small bowl that fits snugly over a saucepan with barely simmering water. Heat until melted. Stir to blend. Or place chocolate in a microwave-safe bowl and microwave on medium for 2 minutes, or until melted. In a mixing bowl cream butter and sugar until light and fluffy. Beat in eggs, vanilla and liqueur or coffee. Stir in chocolate. In a bowl combine the flour, baking powder and salt. Add to the creamed mixture,

mixing until blended. Cut both nuts into halves or thirds and fold in. Divide dough in half. Place on a greased and floured baking sheet and form into two logs about ½ inch thick, 1½ inches wide and 14 inches long, spacing them at least 2 inches apart. Bake in the middle of a preheated 325 degree oven for 25 to 30 minutes or until set and baked through. Transfer from the baking sheet to a rack. Let cool 5 minutes. Place on a cutting board. With a serrated knife slice diagonally at a 45 degree angle about ½ inch thick. Lay the slices flat on the baking sheet and return to a 300 degree oven for 10 to 15 minutes, turning them over once, to dry slightly. Let cool on a rack. Store in a tightly covered container.

Makes about 4 dozen.

White Chocolate Macadamia Biscotti

½ cup butter

¾ cup sugar

2 eggs

1 teaspoon vanilla extract

2 tablespoons Amaretto

2 cups plus 2 tablespoons unbleached or all-purpose flour

1 ½ teaspoons baking powder

¼ teaspoon salt

⅔ cup macadamia nuts

⅔ cup white chocolate chips

Sweet macadamias and white chocolate chips are a felicitous combo in these crisp-tender cookies.

In a mixing bowl cream butter and sugar until light and fluffy. Beat in eggs, vanilla and liqueur. In a bowl combine the flour, baking powder and salt. Add to the creamed mixture, mixing until blended. Fold in nuts and chocolate chips. Divide dough in half. On a greased and floured baking sheet pat out into two logs about ½ inch high, 1 ½ inches wide and 14 inches long, spacing them at least 2 inches apart. Bake in the middle of a preheated 325 degree oven for 25 minutes or until lightly browned. Transfer from baking sheet to a rack. Let cool for 5 minutes. Place on a cutting board. With a serrated knife slice diagonally on a 45 degree angle about ½ inch thick. Place the slices upright on the baking sheet and return to the oven for about 8 minutes longer to dry slightly. Let cool on a rack. Store in a tightly covered container.

Makes about 3 ½ to 4 dozen.

REGIONAL

VARIATIONS

Moorish Apricot Delight

Tangy tender apricots and sweet-meated pistachios lend a chewy bite in this crispy cookie that is scented with the aroma of saffron. Don't go overboard on using the fine filaments; just a touch of this spice lends intrigue while too much brings a medicinal taste.

Sprinkle saffron into orange juice in a small bowl and heat in a preheated 325 degree oven for 5 minutes to infuse the flavor. In a mixing bowl cream butter and sugar until light and fluffy. Beat in eggs and orange juice with saffron. In a bowl combine the flour, baking powder, cloves and salt. Add to the creamed mixture, mixing until blended. Fold in apricots and nuts. Divide dough in half. On a greased and floured baking sheet pat out into two logs about ½ inch high, 1½ inches wide and 14 inches long, spacing them at least 2 inches apart. Bake in the middle of a preheated 325 degree oven for 25 minutes or until lightly browned. Transfer from the baking sheet to a rack. Let cool for 5 minutes. Place on a cutting board. With a serrated knife slice diagonally at a 45 degree angle about ½ inch thick. Place the slices upright on the baking sheet ½ inch apart and return to the oven for 10 minutes longer to dry slightly. Let cool on a rack. Store in a tightly covered container.

Makes about 3½ to 4 dozen.

8 saffron filaments

2 tablespoons orange juice

½ cup butter

¾ cup sugar

2 eggs

2 cups plus 2 tablespoons unbleached or all-purpose flour

1½ teaspoons baking powder

½ teaspoon ground cloves

¼ teaspoon salt

¾ cup apricot halves, finely chopped

⅔ cup pistachio nuts

Biscotti Aloha

1/2 cup butter

3/4 cup sugar

2 eggs

2 tablespoons Coconut
Amaretto or milk and 1/4
teaspoon almond extract

2 cups plus 2 tablespoons
unbleached or all-purpose
flour

1 1/2 teaspoons baking
powder

1/4 teaspoon ground nutmeg

1/4 teaspoon salt

2/3 cup macadamia nuts

1/2 cup shredded coconut

Macadamias and coconut bring the Hawaiian touch to these winning biscotti.

In a mixing bowl cream butter and sugar until light and fluffy. Beat in eggs, Coconut Amaretto or milk, and almond extract. In a bowl combine the flour, baking powder, nutmeg and salt. Add to the creamed mixture, mixing until blended. Fold in nuts and coconut. Divide dough in half. On a greased and floured baking sheet pat out into two logs about 1/2 inch high, 1 1/2 inches wide and 14 inches long, spacing them at least 2 inches apart. Bake in the middle of a preheated 325 degree oven for 25 minutes or until lightly browned. Transfer from the baking sheet to a rack. Let cool for 5 minutes. Place on a cutting board. With a serrated knife slice diagonally on a 45 degree angle about 1/2 inch thick. Lay the slices flat on the baking sheet and return to the oven for 10 minutes longer, turning them over once, to dry slightly. Let cool on a rack. Store in a tightly covered container.

Makes about 3 1/2 to 4 dozen.

Orange Almond Diamonds

This delectable take-off on biscotti is both crunchy and chewy, similar to an orange-flavored almond macaroon. With nuts my passion, far surpassing chocolate, this one is chock-full of goodness.

Place nuts in a shallow pan and bake in a preheated 350 degree oven for 8 to 10 minutes, or until golden brown. Let cool. Place in a food processor fitted with the steel blade and grind until fine but so they still have texture. Set aside. In a mixing bowl beat egg until light and then beat in sugar until pale in color. Add liqueur and orange zest. Toss nuts with cornstarch and salt and mix in. On a greased and floured baking sheet, spread batter into a 7-by-11-inch rectangle. Bake in the middle of a preheated 325 degree oven for 10 minutes or until golden brown. Remove from the oven and transfer to a cutting board. With a sharp knife, cut the cookies lengthwise into four strips, then cut diagonally at a 45 degree angle, making diamonds. Place on the baking sheet. Return to the oven and bake 5 to 6 minutes longer, to dry slightly. Let cool on a rack. Store in a tightly covered container.

Note. Use a vegetable peeler to cut the orange zest into long strips; then chop finely.

Makes about 3 dozen.

1 ½ cups whole blanched almonds

1 egg

¾ cup light brown sugar, packed

1 tablespoon orange liqueur

1 tablespoon finely chopped orange zest

2 tablespoons cornstarch

⅛ teaspoon salt

Candied Orange Pecan Biscotti

1 cup Candied Orange Peel
(recipe follows)

³/₄ cup pecans

¹/₂ cup butter

³/₄ cup sugar

2 eggs

2 tablespoons orange liqueur
or orange juice concentrate,
thawed

Zest of 1 orange, minced
finely

2 cups plus 2 tablespoons all-
purpose or unbleached flour

1¹/₂ teaspoons baking
powder

¹/₄ teaspoon salt

*Bittersweet chunks of candied orange peel and toasted pecans lend a
delicious dimension to these biscotti.*

Prepare candied orange peel and set aside.

To prepare biscotti dough, place nuts in a shallow pan and bake
in a 350 degree oven for 8 to 10 minutes, or until golden brown.
Let cool. In a mixing bowl cream butter and sugar until light and
fluffy. Beat in eggs, orange liqueur, and orange zest. In a bowl
combine the flour, baking powder and salt and mix in just until
blended. Fold in nuts and the Candied Orange Peel. Divide dough
in half. Place on a greased and floured baking sheet and form into
two logs about ¹/₂ inch thick, 1¹/₂ inches wide and 14 inches long,
spacing them at least 2 inches apart. Bake in the middle of a
preheated 325 degree oven for 25 to 30 minutes or until set and
lightly browned. Transfer from the baking sheet to a rack. Let
cool 5 minutes. Place on a cutting board. With a serrated knife
slice diagonally at a 45 degree angle about ¹/₂ inch thick. Place
the slices upright on a baking sheet and return to the oven at
300 degrees for 10 to 15 minutes to dry slightly. Let cool on a
rack. Store in a tightly covered container.

Makes about 3¹/₂ to 4 dozen.

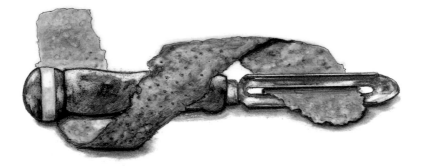

Candied Orange Peel

To prepare Candied Orange Peel, peel oranges, scoring the peel into 5 or 6 sections to make them equal in size. Place the peel in a saucepan, cover with water and simmer 10 minutes. Drain and let cool. With a grapefruit knife, lift off most of the white pith. In a saucepan combine the water and sugar. Bring to a boil and cook until dissolved. Add peel and let simmer until liquid is absorbed, about 45 minutes to 1 hour. Lift peel out onto waxed paper to cool. Makes about 1 cup candied peel.

3 oranges (use peel only)

$\frac{1}{2}$ cup water

$\frac{1}{2}$ cup sugar

Triple Ginger Lovers' Biscotti

¾ cup almonds

½ cup butter

¾ cup dark brown sugar, firmly packed

2 tablespoons molasses

2 eggs

2 ¼ cups all-purpose flour

2 teaspoons ground ginger

1 ½ teaspoons baking powder

¼ teaspoon salt

2 tablespoons chopped fresh ginger root

⅔ cup finely chopped crystallized ginger

Three styles of ginger—powdered, fresh and candied—permeate these spicy cookies.

Place nuts in a shallow pan and bake in a 350 degree oven for 8 to 10 minutes, or until golden brown. Let cool. In a mixing bowl cream butter and sugar until light and fluffy. Beat in molasses and eggs. In another bowl combine the flour, ground ginger, baking powder and salt. Add to the creamed mixture, mixing until blended. Stir in fresh and crystallized ginger. Cut nuts into halves or thirds and fold in. Divide dough in half. Place on an ungreased baking sheet and form into two logs about ½ inch thick, 1 ½ inches wide and 14 inches long, spacing them at least 2 inches apart. Bake in the middle of a preheated 325 degree oven for 25 minutes or until a light golden brown. Transfer from the baking sheet to a rack. Let cool 5 minutes. Place on a cutting board. With a serrated knife slice diagonally at a 45 degree angle about ½ inch thick. Lay the slices flat on the baking sheet and return to the oven for 10 minutes, turning them over once, to dry slightly. Let cool on a rack. Store in a tightly covered container.

Makes about 3 ½ dozen biscotti.

Almond Crunch Biscotti

Slices of caramelized almonds ribbon these biscotti.

To prepare Caramelized Almond Slices, in a skillet melt butter with sugar. When it bubbles and just starts to turn golden add almonds and continue cooking, shaking pan to prevent from burning, until nuts turn golden and caramelized. Turn out on a baking sheet and let cool. Break into pieces.

To prepare biscotti dough, in a mixing bowl cream butter and sugar until light and fluffy. Beat in eggs and vanilla. In a bowl combine the flour, baking powder, soda and salt. Add to the creamed mixture, mixing just until blended. Stir in Caramelized Almond Slices. Divide dough in half. On a greased and floured baking sheet pat out into two logs about ¹/₂ inch high, 1 ¹/₂ inches wide and 14 inches long, spacing them at least 2 inches apart. Bake in the middle of a preheated 325 degree oven for 25 minutes or until lightly browned. Transfer from the baking sheet to a rack. Let cool for 5 minutes. Place on a cutting board. With a serrated knife slice diagonally at a 45 degree angle about ³/₈ inch thick. Lay the slices flat on the baking sheet and return to the oven for 10 minutes, turning them over once, to dry slightly. Let cool on a rack. Store in a tightly covered container.

Makes about 3 ¹/₂ to 4 dozen.

Caramelized Almond Slices:

2 tablespoons butter

3 tablespoons sugar

³/₄ cup sliced blanched almonds

Biscotti dough:

¹/₂ cup butter

³/₄ cup sugar

2 eggs

1 teaspoon vanilla extract

2 cups unbleached or all-purpose flour

1 teaspoon baking powder

¹/₄ teaspoon baking soda

¹/₄ teaspoon salt

Pistachio and Golden Raisin Biscotti

1/2 cup butter

1 cup plus 2 tablespoons sugar

3 eggs, separated

1 1/2 teaspoons vanilla extract

2 teaspoons grated lemon zest

3 cups all-purpose or unbleached flour

2 teaspoons baking powder

1/4 teaspoon salt

1 1/4 cups shelled whole pistachio nuts

1 1/4 cups golden raisins

3 to 4 ounces white chocolate (optional)

Pistachios and golden raisins nugget these cookies, which can have a stripe of white chocolate.

In a mixing bowl cream butter and 1/2 cup sugar until light and fluffy. Beat in egg yolks, vanilla extract and lemon zest. In a bowl combine flour, baking powder and salt and add to the creamed mixture, mixing just until crumbly. In a separate bowl beat egg whites until soft peaks form and beat in remaining sugar, beating until stiff but not dry. Fold meringue into the crumbly dough, mixing until it clings together. Fold in nuts and raisins. Divide dough in half. Form into two logs on a greased and floured baking sheet, making them about 1/2 inch thick, 1 1/2 inches wide and 16 inches long, spacing them at least 2 inches apart. Bake in the middle of a preheated 325 degree oven for 25 to 30 minutes or until set and golden brown. Transfer from the baking sheet to a rack. Let cool 5 minutes. Place on a cutting board. With a serrated

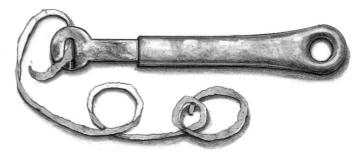

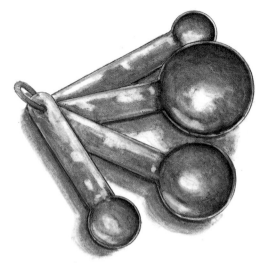

knife slice diagonally at a 45 degree angle into ½ inch slices. Place the slices upright on a baking sheet and return to the oven at 300 degrees for 10 to 15 minutes to dry slightly. Let cool on a rack. Store in a tightly covered container.

Chocolate Glaze variation: Place the chocolate in a small bowl that fits snugly over a saucepan of barely simmering water. Heat until chocolate melts. Stir to blend. Or place chocolate in a microwave-safe bowl and microwave on medium about 2 minutes, or until melted. Stir to blend. Spread chocolate with a spatula over entire top surface of cookies. Let cool at room temperature until set.

Makes about 4 dozen.

Mandelbrot

2/3 cup blanched whole
almonds

1/3 cup butter

3/4 cup sugar

3 eggs

1 tablespoon grated lemon
zest

2 tablespoons lemon juice

2 cups plus 2 tablespoons
unbleached or all-purpose
flour

1 teaspoon baking powder

1/4 teaspoon baking soda

1/4 teaspoon salt

*These Jewish-style twice-baked cookies have many variations, among
them, candied fruit and chocolate sprinkles sometimes stipple the
slices. The name translates as "almond bread" in Yiddish.*

Place nuts in a shallow pan and bake in a 350 degree oven for
8 to 10 minutes, or until golden brown. Let cool. In a mixing
bowl cream butter and sugar until light and fluffy. Beat in eggs,
lemon zest and juice. In a bowl combine the flour, baking powder, soda and salt. Add to the creamed mixture, mixing just until
blended. Cut nuts into halves or thirds and fold in. Divide dough
in half. On a greased and floured baking sheet pat out into two
logs about 1/2 inch high, 1 1/2 inches wide and 14 inches long,
spacing at least 2 inches apart. Bake in the middle of a preheated
325 degree oven for 25 minutes or until lightly browned. Transfer
from the baking sheet to a rack. Let cool for 5 minutes. Place on
a cutting board. With a serrated knife slice diagonally at a 45 degree angle about 1/2 inch thick. Place the slices upright 1/2 inch
apart on the baking sheet and return to the oven for 10 minutes
longer to dry slightly. Let cool on a rack. Store in a tightly
covered container.

Makes about 3 1/2 to 4 dozen.

Praline Biscotti

Praline:

1/3 cup sugar

1/3 cup slivered blanched almonds

Biscotti dough:

2/3 cup whole almonds

1/2 cup butter

2/3 cup sugar

2 eggs

1 teaspoon vanilla extract

2 cups plus 2 tablespoons unbleached or all-purpose flour

1 1/2 teaspoons baking powder

1/4 teaspoon salt

Almond candy crystals fleck these cookies with their sublime, shattering sweetness.

To prepare Praline, place sugar in a heavy saucepan over moderate heat, shaking pan, until sugar melts and caramelizes. Add almonds and shake to coat nuts, then immediately pour mixture out of the pan onto a buttered sheet of foil. Let cool. Break candy into pieces and pulverize in a blender into a fine powder.

To prepare biscotti dough, place nuts in a shallow pan and bake in a preheated 350 degree oven for 8 to 10 minutes, or until golden brown. Let cool. In a mixing bowl cream butter and sugar until light and fluffy. Beat in eggs and vanilla. In a bowl combine the flour, baking powder, and salt. Add to the creamed mixture, mixing until blended. Stir in Praline. Cut almonds into halves or thirds and fold in. Divide dough in half. On a greased and floured baking sheet pat out into two logs about 1/2 inch high, 1 1/2 inches wide and 14 inches long, spacing them at least 2 inches apart. Bake in the middle of a preheated 325 degree oven for 25 minutes or until lightly browned. Transfer from baking sheet to a rack. Let cool for 5 minutes. Place on a cutting board. With a serrated knife slice diagonally at a 45 degree angle about 1/2 inch thick. Lay the slices cut side down on the baking sheet and return to the oven for 10 minutes, turning them over once, to dry slightly. Let cool on a rack. Store in a tightly covered container.

Makes about 3 1/2 to 4 dozen.

Espresso Biscotti

Ground dark roast coffee beans lend a haunting espresso flavor here. These are neat paired with a coffee beverage—cappuccino or caffelatte.

Place nuts in a shallow pan and bake in a preheated 350 degree oven for 7 to 8 minutes, or until golden brown. Let cool. Grind coffee beans into a fine powder. Place in a small bowl, add Kahlua or coffee and heat in a preheated 325 degree oven for 5 to 7 minutes to steep. Or place in a microwave-safe dish, add Kahlua or coffee and microwave on high 10 to 15 seconds to steep. Set aside. In a mixing bowl cream butter and sugar until light and fluffy. Beat in eggs and ground coffee and liqueur. In a bowl combine the flour, baking powder and salt. Add to the creamed mixture, mixing until blended. Fold in nuts. Divide dough in half. On a greased and floured baking sheet pat out into two logs about $1/2$ inch high, $1 1/2$ inches wide and 14 inches long, spacing them at least 2 inches apart. Bake in the middle of a preheated 325 degree oven for 25 minutes or until lightly browned. Transfer from the baking sheet to a rack. Let cool for 5 minutes. Place on a cutting board. With a serrated knife slice diagonally at a 45 degree angle about $1/2$ inch thick. Place the slices upright on the baking sheet $1/2$ inch apart and return to the oven for 10 minutes longer to dry slightly. Let cool on a rack. Store in a tightly covered container.

Makes about 3 $1/2$ to 4 dozen.

$2/3$ cup blanched slivered almonds

3 tablespoons coffee beans

2 tablespoons Kahlua or double-strength coffee

$1/2$ cup butter

$3/4$ cup sugar

2 eggs

2 cups plus 2 tablespoons unbleached or all-purpose flour

$1 1/2$ teaspoons baking powder

$1/4$ teaspoon salt

Swedish Cinnamon Slices

2/3 cup blanched slivered almonds

1 cup butter

1 cup light brown sugar, packed

2 eggs

2 tablespoons sour cream

1/2 teaspoon almond extract

2 3/4 cups unbleached or all-purpose flour

1 tablespoon cinnamon

1 teaspoon baking powder

1/4 teaspoon soda

1/4 teaspoon salt

This Scandinavian favorite is subtle, with cinnamon spicing up its crisp-tender texture.

Place nuts in a shallow pan and bake in a 350 degree oven for 6 to 8 minutes, or until golden brown. Let cool. In a mixing bowl cream butter and sugar until light and fluffy. Beat in eggs, sour cream and almond extract. In a bowl combine the flour, cinnamon, baking powder, soda and salt. Add to the creamed mixture, mixing until blended. Fold in nuts. Divide dough in half. On a greased and floured baking sheet pat out into two logs about

½ inch high, 1½ inches wide and 15 inches long, spacing them at least 2 inches apart. Bake in the middle of a preheated 350 degree oven for 20 to 25 minutes or until lightly browned. Remove from the baking sheet to a rack. Let cool for 5 minutes. Place on a cutting board. With a serrated knife slice diagonally at a 45 degree angle about ½ inch thick. Place the slices upright on the baking sheet ½ inch apart and return to a 325 degree oven for 10 minutes longer to dry slightly. Let cool on a rack. Store in a tightly covered container.

Makes about 3½ to 4 dozen.

HEALTHFUL

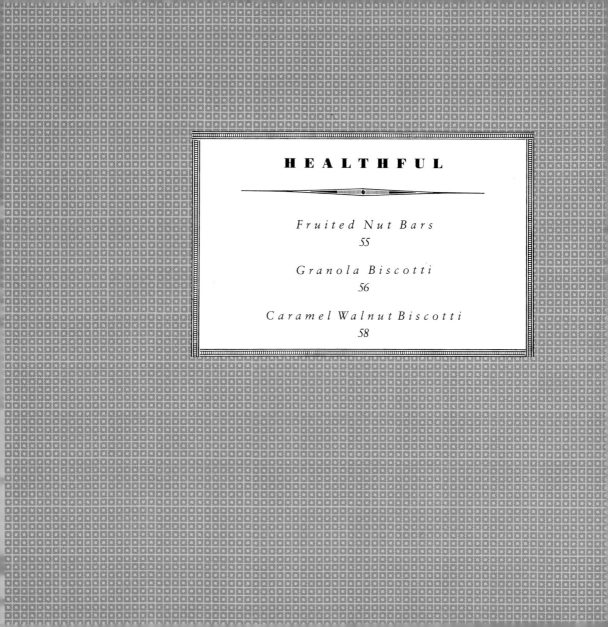

Fruited Nut Bars
55

Granola Biscotti
56

Caramel Walnut Biscotti
58

Fruited Nut Bars

Made with whole wheat flour, this whole grain fruit bar is a nourishing backpack or breakfast snack. It is excellent with various dried fruits: figs, dates or apricots.

Place nuts in a shallow pan and bake in a preheated 325 degree oven for 8 to 10 minutes, or until golden brown. Let cool. In a mixing bowl cream butter and sugar until light and fluffy. Beat in eggs and vanilla. In a bowl combine the flour, baking powder, salt, cinnamon, cloves and allspice. Add to the creamed mixture, mixing until blended. Coarsely chop nuts and fold in. Stir in fruit. Divide dough in half. On a greased and floured baking sheet pat out into two logs about 1/2 inch high, 1 1/2 inches wide and 14 inches long, spacing them at least 2 inches apart. Bake in the middle of a preheated 325 degree oven for 25 minutes or until lightly browned. Transfer from the baking sheet to a rack. Let cool for 5 minutes. Place on a cutting board. With a serrated knife slice diagonally at a 45 degree angle about 1/2 inch thick. Place the slices upright on the baking sheet and return to the oven for 10 minutes longer to dry slightly. Let cool on a rack. Store in a tightly covered container.

Makes about 3 1/2 to 4 dozen.

2/3 cup walnuts or pecans

1/2 cup butter

1 cup light brown sugar, packed

2 eggs

1 teaspoon vanilla extract

2 cups whole wheat flour

1 1/2 teaspoons baking powder

1/4 teaspoon salt

2 teaspoons cinnamon

1/4 teaspoon ground cloves

1/4 teaspoon ground allspice

3/4 cup chopped figs, dates or dried apricots

Granola Biscotti

1 cup granola (recipe follows)

²/₃ cup blanched sliced almonds

¹/₂ cup butter

²/₃ cup light brown sugar, packed

¹/₃ cup honey

2 eggs

1 teaspoon vanilla extract

2 cups unbleached or all-purpose flour

1 teaspoon baking powder

¹/₄ teaspoon baking soda

1 ¹/₂ teaspoons cinnamon

¹/₄ teaspoon salt

The popular breakfast snack granola imparts a wholesome oat crunch to these cookies.

Prepare the granola and set aside.

To prepare biscotti dough, place nuts in a shallow pan and bake in a preheated 325 degree oven for 8 to 10 minutes, or until golden brown. Let cool. In a mixing bowl cream butter and sugar until light and fluffy. Beat in honey, eggs and vanilla. In a bowl combine the flour, baking powder, soda, cinnamon and salt. Add to the creamed mixture, mixing until blended.

Mix in granola and nuts. Divide dough in half. On a greased and floured baking sheet pat out into two logs about ¹/₂ inch high, 1 ¹/₂ inches wide and 14 inches long, spacing at least 2 inches apart. Bake in the middle of a preheated 325 degree oven for 25 minutes or until lightly browned. Transfer from the baking sheet to a rack. Let cool for 5 minutes. Place on a cutting board. With a serrated knife slice diagonally at a 45 degree angle about ³/₈ inch thick. Lay the slices flat on the baking sheet and return to the oven for 10 minutes longer, turning them over once, to dry slightly. Let cool on a rack. Store in a tightly covered container.

Makes about 4 dozen.

Granola

To prepare Granola, place in a small saucepan the oil, honey, sugar and vanilla. Heat, stirring, just until combined. Spread oatmeal in a shallow baking pan. Pour the honey mixture over the oatmeal and mix until well coated. Bake in a preheated 325 degree oven for 30 minutes, or until oatmeal is slightly crisp and lightly browned, stirring twice. Let cool.

Or place the oil, honey, sugar and vanilla in a microwave-safe bowl. Microwave on high for 30 seconds to heat through. Spread oatmeal in a shallow baking dish. Pour the honey mixture over the oatmeal and mix until well coated. Microwave on high for 2 minutes; stir. Microwave 3 to 5 minutes longer or until the oatmeal is slightly crisp and lightly browned. Let cool.

Makes 1 cup.

1 ¹/₂ tablespoons olive oil or vegetable oil

1 ¹/₂ tablespoons honey

1 ¹/₂ tablespoons brown sugar, packed

¹/₂ teaspoon vanilla extract

1 cup regular oatmeal

Caramel Walnut Biscotti

3/4 cup walnuts

1/2 cup finely ground oatmeal

1/2 cup butter

3/4 cup dark brown sugar, packed

2 eggs

2 tablespoons Kahlua or double-strength coffee

1 teaspoon vanilla extract

1 3/4 cups unbleached or all-purpose flour

1 1/2 teaspoons baking powder

1/4 teaspoon salt

Dark brown sugar and Kahlua produce a caramelized flavor in these toasted walnut biscotti that are enriched with oat flour. Oat flour is quickly made by grinding oatmeal in a blender or a food processor.

Place nuts in a shallow pan and bake in a preheated 350 degree oven for 8 to 10 minutes, or until golden brown. Let cool. Place oat flour in a baking pan and bake in a 350 degree oven for 8 to 10 minutes, or until golden brown. In a mixing bowl cream butter and sugar until light and fluffy. Beat in eggs, Kahlua or coffee, and vanilla. In a bowl combine the flour, baking powder and salt. Add to the creamed mixture, mixing just until blended. Mix in oat flour. Coarsely chop nuts and fold in. Divide dough in half. On a greased and floured baking sheet pat out into two logs about 1/2 inch high, 1 1/2 inches wide and 14 inches long, spacing at least 2 inches apart. Bake in the middle of a preheated 325 degree oven for 25 minutes or until lightly browned. Transfer from baking sheet to a rack. Let cool for 5 minutes. Place on a cutting board. With a serrated knife slice diagonally on a 45 degree angle about 1/2 inch thick. Lay the slices flat on the baking sheet and return to the oven for 10 minutes, turning them over once, to dry slightly. Let cool on a rack. Store in a tightly covered container.

Makes about 3 1/2 to 4 dozen.

Index of Recipes